SOON IT WILL BE SUNDAY

ALSO BY LANG LEAV

Poetry & Prose

Love and Misadventure

Lullabies

Memories

The Universe of Us

Sea of Strangers

Love Looks Pretty on You

September Love

The Gift of Everything

Self-Love for Small-Town Girls

Hello Lovely!

Fiction

Sad Girls

Poemsia

Others Were Emeralds

For Whiskey

The authorised representative in the EEA is Simon and Schuster Netherlands BV, Herculesplein 96 3584 AA Utrecht, Netherlands. (info@simonandschuster.nl)

Andrews McMeel Publishing
a division of Andrews McMeel Universal
1130 Walnut Street, Kansas City, Missouri 64106

www.andrewsmcmeel.com

25 26 27 28 29 VEP 10 9 8 7 6 5 4 3 2 1

ISBN: 979-8-8816-0011-2

Library of Congress Control Number: 2025937741

Editor: Melissa R. Zahorsky
Art Director: Diane Marsh
Production Editor: Dave Shaw
Production Manager: Shona Burns

ATTENTION: SCHOOLS AND BUSINESSES
Andrews McMeel books are available at quantity discounts with bulk purchase for educational, business, or sales promotional use. For information, please e-mail the Andrews McMeel Publishing Special Sales Department: sales@andrewsmcmeel.com.

SOON IT WILL BE SUNDAY

LANG LEAV

With You

At this juncture, where there is more behind me than beyond, I think of everything I have touched. I regret all the things I should have done for the ones I loved. In this life, I wish I had done more than I have. You don't know how fast it all goes or that, in the end, this will be the only thing that matters.

When you get to where I am, all you want to know is: Was there someone? Just one person whom you could look in the eye and say, *with you, I did everything right.*

Beacon

I am a beacon of my own happiness.

Houses

We lived in more than a dozen houses that year. Cast out from our birthright. Sheltered in place. Left to figure out light switches and extraneous delivery apps. Dreaming of laundry powder, dentist appointments, grocery lists, longing for home. Our listless fingers tapping out words that came in the dead of night like long-buried dreams. Baffled by our predicament. We were walking on eggshells or jumping through hoops. It felt there was no end to the labyrinth. We suffered but there was beauty too, as in everything. One day, from a place you couldn't reach me, you watched helpless, as I threw myself into the arms of the ocean. That was when I learned to swim. When I made peace with uncertainty and found a home there.

Salt Mill

How much salt goes in the pan?
I do not know the quantity,
no point of measurement
or reference.

With the salt mill in my hand,
I do not know how many turns
of the wrist it takes,
only that my hands
know exactly when to stop.

This Part of My Life

By the sea, you are cradled in the warm golden womb of the shore. The afternoon sun spills molten light, blessing everything with its soft, eternal glow. You close your eyes and murmur, *just for a moment.*

The moment passes and you are roused by a gust of wind, chilling you to the bone. You blink, bewildered by the dwindling light, the sun all but gone. It feels like I am in this part of my life.

Offering

For the women of Bali

We arrange flowers for my daylight offering,
neatly ordered, like keeping time: frangipani,
marigold, ylang-ylang, and hibiscus.
My guide, Oshin, says, *this is canang sari.*
She dresses me in a ceremonial sarong,
shows me how to kneel in reverence
at this ancient place I have come to,
where time lapses into memory,
my palms turned upward to the sky,
where holy water drips from my fingers.
She says, *here we cultivate our gardens*
to appease the gods, in gratitude,
we sow and bear and bloom, toil in their honor.
When Oshin speaks the name of the sun god Surya,
He comes surging through the clouds,
His face an orb of such astonishing light
even the hummingbird is stilled—I see
a hand reaching across the threshold
of existence, ever searching for mine.
At the altar before me, I place my offering.

Written about my experiences during my stay
at Alila, Uluwatu.

Sea Fog

From the paint chips fanned across
the counter, we are asked to pick
from a kaleidoscope of white,
from stark, cold alabaster
to rich, butterscotch creams
when the shade *seafog* catches my eye,
and the clarity of feeling strikes me
clean through to the heart.
To think, our walls will be painted
with this feeling.

Soon It Will Be Sunday

On a perfect Monday morning, I am already self-destructing. It is only the start of the week, but it feels like the end.

You say, *we still have until Sunday, and then, we have the rest of our lives.*

But soon it will be Sunday and you'll be getting on that plane.

Soon it will be Sunday and I'm going to lose you forever.

You could never lose me, you say, but you're wrong about that.

People are the easiest thing to lose.

Synchronicity

While I am yet to fully grasp the concept of synchronicity, based on my experiences, I've noticed a correlation between its frequency and the occurrence of wonderful things in my life.

Never Without You

Would my life
have been different
without you?

I can never know
for I was never
without you.

Immortality

I will make you immortal in the way of poets and vampires. Haunt the darkest corners of your memories. Appear before you as you are doomscrolling down the endless abyss, tripping into rabbit holes, finding me in places you never thought I'd be. You will recognize the words, see yourself as in a mirror. Feel the burning heat of my attention for that one glorious moment, knowing you could have had me for as long as you wanted. Through me, you can live on forever. But only if I say your name.

Enough

I love you. We love each other.
That should be enough.
I don't know why it isn't.

The Creative Life

Some people live their lives, moment to moment, year by year. Defined by anniversaries and milestones. For me, it's project to project. Each creative endeavor sets its own schedule, has its own life force, its own universe that pulls me in, sets me on a timeline. This mysterious, benevolent force puts me on a path and will only release me when it's done, even when I'm not ready to say goodbye. But before I have a chance to mourn the loss, I am hit with another spark of inspiration, charged with another idea to carefully nurture and bring to fruition. I can't imagine living any other way than this, the ever-present impulse to put something beautiful into the world. To have the privilege of repeating this process. How empty my life would be otherwise.

Nothing Is as Fleeting

Wonderstruck, sleepwalking into
this maddening love,
I saw a light unlike any other.
Under the guise of anonymity,
Venus and the crescent moon,
I walked through hellfire
to find you, to be with you.
I would burn for all eternity
if I could stay here for the night,
stay until every star burns out,
but even stars are finite.
You can say forever, if you want to,
but you and I both know,
nothing is as fleeting.

Women Who Want Will Say

When you subtract from everything,
all you have left is time.

They say,
we do not want more–
we want less
and to be happy with that.

Silent

Because I was trying to tell you something that I've been waiting all day to tell you, something that meant so damn much to me, but in that crucial moment, you were distracted, your attention was elsewhere and so I took a breath and fell silent.

Redirection

At the appropriate time, I would impress on you the urgency of intervening when you sense certain disaster for a beloved friend—steering them from their doomed course before it's too late. Throw everything you can, even if they are the one fighting you the hardest, even if no one else agrees. Sometimes, you're the only one in a position to derail what was never meant for them, knock the poisoned chalice from their hand, ground the plane as they stand by the runway, clutching their suitcase. Stop the ring from slipping onto their finger, stand up and speak your mind. The most gracious thing you can do is move the universe for somebody you love in the hopes they may someday do the same for you.

The Process

The process of writing acts as a coagulant. Find your words where the wound still gushes.

The Ocean Never Stops Asking

In the summer of '97,
when day after day,
the sun beamed down its fury,
I was seventeen, tired of seeking refuge
from the incendiary heat
in the air-conditioned cool
of a Westfield shopping mall,
two train stops away from Cabramatta.
When my friend said, we'd go to Cronulla.
Can you imagine the audacity!
Us, treading on the sanctity
of their white sand beach,
an aberration among
their white, tanned bodies,
our foreign faces stinging
from their proverbial taunts,
go back to where you came from,
rubbing salt in our tender wounds.
Yet we persisted, seduced by the cool,
bubbling waves, the tickle of a breeze.
Bravely, we stepped over fault lines
between the bitumen and the shore,
between southwest Sydney and the Shire,
we crossed the threshold into the water
to be baptized by this country we loved
more fiercely than we were allowed,
this continent squelched into a misshapen heart.
In Siem Reap, on the Tonlé Sap River,
Dad lived in a house, perched on stilts,

from the bamboo planks of the makeshift deck,
he'd jump straight into the water,
to the water, he'd lost so much
but the ocean never stops asking.
I grab a fistful of sand, perfect and golden,
and place it into the mouth of the sea.

In my poem "The Ocean Never Stops Asking," I reflect on a quintessentially Australian pastime: a day at the beach. However, for children of immigrants in the 90s, this ordinary activity could be fraught with tension. Cronulla beach, famous for being accessible by train, proved irresistible to teens seeking relief from the blistering heat of an Aussie summer. Still, the beach had an undercurrent of danger well before the eruption of the 2005 riots. Yet we continued to flock there, drawn to the water by an innate, primal urge, undeterred by the open hostility of the locals.

After all, we were no strangers to peril, having grown up in a suburb dubbed as the drug capital of Australia. But for all its faults, Cabramatta was also a place of refuge and belonging—a contradiction I explore in my recent novel *Others Were Emeralds*. Like my characters, my friends and I were regular teens, preoccupied with schoolwork, crushes, and peer groups. Unlike typical teenagers, we were the children of refugees who had come from war-torn countries and suffered unimaginable horrors.

For much of its terrifying reign, the Khmer Rouge destroyed photographs in an attempt to erase the past. Consequently, I have never seen pictures of my parents before the war. I can only grasp fragments of my family's history through the stories they tell.

One such story, told by my father, paints a vivid picture of his childhood home. He describes how, for half the year, the patch of dirt under his stilt house remained dry and barren until the monsoon came and the Mekong River swelled, filling up the adjoining rivers. A body of water would appear beneath him as if by magic, transforming his cherished boyhood home into an idyllic playground. I often imagine the ramshackle house on stilts, standing proud and sturdy before the devastation of Pol Pot and his killing fields. I picture my father as a boy, just on the cusp of manhood, poised to jump.

The Guardian *(Australia) first published this poem and essay as part of Red Room's Poetry Month.*

Lines

Your smile, a line
snagging on every mouth.

Your heart—cold, anatomical,
a thin, quivering line
on a cardiogram.

I make the bed for us.
There is a crease that goes
from my side to yours.
You can call it a line, I guess.
Every poem ends with one.

Pretenses

Don't tell me who you are. Tell me what you've done and that will tell me everything.

Creativity

Creativity is born from chaos but thrives in the mundane. When inspiration strikes, you may not be in the best place to bring it to fruition. You may be going through things that need your immediate and constant attention. But do not despair for ideas are not governed by the passage of time. So, wait for the right conditions. Wait until you find your center and get your bearings. When you can settle into a routine. That's when the magic happens.

Parts

Who do you keep comparing me to in your head—these wistful criticisms that have only just emerged, the idea you're stuck on about this ideal version of me that doesn't exist and never will? Whatever you want, it's no longer this, not in its entirety. But there are still parts you can't stand to lose. Like something cold and unfeeling, a car engine or a refrigerator, you keep me for my parts.

Showing Up

I was present that warm, balmy night, in a way I hadn't been in such a long time. I stood under the blazing night sky, electrified by my own aliveness, every fiber of my skin, alight. It was akin to falling in love, as though I had arrived in some small way to a moment, a place that had been marked for me. As though God himself had wedged this turn of events into my life for a reason, had made me see what I had been resisting. Revealed to me when I least expected that life can still astonish me. As long as I keep showing up.

The Beauty of Writing

Day after day, you approach the blank page with all your terror and apprehension, despite proving your anxieties wrong time and again. Still, you'd rather be doing anything else, anything to delay the inevitable. Times like this, you must force yourself to write, even if it is just one word. Sometimes a word is all it takes to open the floodgates, for something to take over and then you—not quite knowing how—will feel the words surging, as though a dam has burst somewhere in the center of your soul. This is the beauty of writing.

As a Poet

As a poet, I feel it all at once. This is the only way I know how to be. I am both the heart and the heartbreak, the one who leaves but never does.

The jilted lover and the knife in the back.

With Nothing

You made my life empty, so you'd be the only thing in it. And then you filled yours up to the brim and left me with nothing.

How Much of You Is Here

Between the walls of this old house,
I consider what has passed
through the heat of your hands.

Does the moth-eaten throw still hold
the static charge of your touch?
Does the door of our bedroom
remember how it feels
to be flung wide open?

And what of the mulberry wine stain
on the kitchen counter—
does it know how much
blood was spilled between us?

Or the box I had marked *fragile.*
The one you carried in from our front porch,
was it ever handled with such care?

I go on listing all the things
you have graced with your fingertips,
pressed your body against on a whim.
When will the time come
when I am all that's left?

With Impunity

To love a creative person means to allow them to fully embrace their art. To step back and encourage them to do their work with full impunity, let them put their creative soul above your own insecurities and understand they don't have to justify the core of their inspiration to you or anyone else.

Lighthouses

Jagged rocks, a siren's call,
we are the saddest part of every story,
the shipwreck of every scene.
We are seas apart and lighthouses for each other,
a confluence of distance and danger,
one splendid eye gazing into the ether—
another searching, always searching.
We are the tide throwing ourselves onto the shore,
to be wrestled back, full of longing.
We are outstretched fingers and acrobats plunging,
barely touching, never holding.

Sinking Ship

It felt like a slow disintegration, as though watching myself from afar aboard a sinking ship. I want to scream, *jump*. I want to say, *get out before it's too late*. But I don't.

By Touch

In the dark, I reach into my drawer with intention. I know the exact size, shape, texture, and weight of the item I seek. I don't turn on the light—there is no need to see what I am looking for. There are certain things we know by touch. People we reach for in the dark, with that same depth of knowing.

Whiskey

At his post, by the bedroom window, our dog Whiskey would watch the sun sink into the ocean. Day after day, he was there, like clockwork, his expression a practiced calm, tinged with melancholy, so very human. A quirk that we got used to seeing at the end of our day, served as a reminder to pause for that tiny miracle, a distraction from the run-of-the-mill, the folding of laundry, attending to the gutters and the wasp nests and the flowers, the school run, the multitude of bills, the sequence of our busy lives, writing at my desk, a wet nose pushed into my hand, at the kitchen stove, stirring a pot, a little body pressed against my leg, a tail wagging, large eyes imploring. A ball of joy that pinballed, around our house, smashing into everything. The years grew wild around us, in the twisted trees, the empty nest—we noticed tiny white flecks appearing on Whiskey's chin, looked into the mirror and saw time reflected in ourselves. And that visit to the vet, it was only meant to be a routine check-up, a few standard tests, just to be sure. But they had found something sinister, had to get to it right away, asked us to say goodbye in case he didn't make it. And late into that afternoon, as we waited by the phone, we stared at his empty bed, baffled and shell-shocked, it seemed to us, implausible the sun could ever set without him. And for the first time in a while, we bowed our heads in prayer, asked if we could have him home one last time, see him in situ, when God answered. Gave us four precious months with our boy, as every day we resolved to impress on him how much he was loved. Whiskey who bounded into the ocean, dove into lakes, tore through the forest, greeted us every morning with such exuberance, to see him quietly resting his head on our laps, eyes full of devotion, it was almost too much to bear. When it was time to say goodbye, his abrupt absence weighed heavy as the sinking sun, our chests battered from the ricocheting grief, when we mourned all the years that had died alongside him.

I Dreamt

I recall a dream where I was on my way to see you.
And in that strangely lucid state I'd thought,
what a sweet and simple thing to want
and how impossible it was.

Incomplete

It is not finished,
it is not complete:
this life,
this love,
this book,
this poem.

Second Migration

My love was like a second migration, a trip to unknown lands. I ventured and was given at the threshold, a new set of eyes, a fresh set of lips, a new pulse. I was taught to be ashamed of who I was, from where I came. All aspects of myself had to be cast aside, made anew. Redressed like a bed or a lampshade or an ideal. Slowly, I emerged, as the thing that I am, no longer recognizable to anyone who once knew me. I stepped into this twisted fairytale. The transformation complete, shut away in my tower, never to return to myself.

Unpacking

In the great unpacking
of our lives, we find remnants of
the life we built together,
and the way we lived it.
Hotel slips, and electricity bills,
novelty cards and funeral notices.
Gifts we bought each other
that we forgot to give.
A set of knives, razor sharp.
Cohen's *Book of Longing*.
Trinkets and denominations
from faraway places.
Articles in magazines
where I am asked about love.
A photo your mother took of us,
back when everything was new,
my head on your shoulder,
our besotted expressions.
Our cats only kittens.
The amalgamation of our books.
the dust from all the years,
and things we couldn't bear
to throw away—it says a lot about us,
our willingness to remain in this place,
with our things and each other.

A Letter to My Mother at Immigration

You will make a life here,
like a wave carving out
the side of a rock.
You will make fossils of your memories
for your daughter to find.

They will change your name;
your daughter will call you
by the one you are reassigned
And you will gladly answer to this name
in exchange for the simple promise

that your daughter will be safe here
But she will not speak your language,
she will not understand you,
and she will deem you incomprehensible.

Yet, you will try to hold her
as she turns away from you
in sharp, painful increments
like the second hand of a clock.
Your daughter will be lost to you.
But do not despair—
for in the blink of an eye,
she will come back to you
with her sad, eloquent stories
and no way to tell you.

You will make a life here,
but it will not be yours.
Your daughter will never consider this truth
until one day, at the edge of the ocean,
she will sense its vastness.

"A Letter to My Mother at Immigration" first appeared on Red Room Poetry commissioned as part of Poetry Month, 2024.

Into Place

Don't worry, you said. *Everything will be okay—you'll see. In time, everything will fall into place.* And you were right. Things did fall into place. Only your place wasn't with me.

Fractured

Here we are
ten years in
love in reverse.

The mirror of my heart
you broke
and fractured
into verse.

Free Will

I would have thought by now
the questions would have all been answered.
Yet, there are still things I want to know.
Was I always fated to find you?
And why did they put everything in our way?

If I had chosen you instead,
would that have altered
the course of our histories?
Would we have been happy?
Did I make the right choice?
Was it even mine to make?

True Love

How was I to know when I turned up at your house, starved of love, that I would drink the cupful you so readily gave, even knowing it was laced with poison? I was dying of loneliness in the way only a person who has been alone could understand, my body straining with want, my throat scratched raw with the heat of my longing. How was I to know that merely steps away from you, true love was waiting for me behind the next door?

My Saving Grace

I have made so many bad decisions in my life, but you were the only thing I had to get right. I chose you, and that has been my saving grace.

Depth of Love

Love does not grow outward,
like a sapling gently unfurling.
It goes inward like the roots of a tree,
piercing deeper and deeper.

And when you burrow into this
dark and dangerous place,
you find things about yourself,
things about your man–
uncut gems and buried bones.

First printed in Notes on Love, *Fenton, 2020.*

Every Rose

You hold the person I love hostage,
you wear his weary face.
I can't seem to comprehend
your hands the way I used to.
There is a disconnect between
your words and their intentions.
Once you said, *every rose dies petal by petal*
and these quiet amputations, this slow death—
this is how it feels to love you.

Ideals

You have this ideal in your head, this picture of how it's meant to be. You spend your whole life getting to that point. You never think beyond it because deep inside, you don't truly believe you'll ever get there. And then you do, but it's not the solution you had hoped for. And suddenly you have to make a whole new picture.

A Place Where Everything Is

I want a place where everything is:
my scraps of paper and cupful of coins.
An overgrown garden for me to meander
dreaming my intrepid dreams, scattered
like breadcrumbs over the roots of trees,
insects moving about in the earth unseen.
A place with you and our borrowed time,
where only the wind knocks on our door.
And there is no need to worry yet,
not until the cat paws staunchly at my cheek,
like a clock hand foreshadowing doom—
not until the hours run into the afternoon.
Not until a thousand setting suns
paint the sky in candy-colored hues,
and I'm left with the ghost of your laughter
lulling me from room to room.

The Mānuka Tree

Late one evening, a storm tore through my garden, sudden and vicious. The wind roared long into the restless night, rattling windows and banging shutters. I thought about the woods outside my house, the tītokis and pohutukawas, the mānuka tree by my bedroom window. The creatures that inhabited the forest, the gurgling tūīs and silvereyes, their tiny birdwings beating. The wildflowers blooming for the bees and butterflies.

I rose early the next morning, steeled myself for the damage and was relieved to find my garden largely unscathed when I noticed to my dismay, the mānuka tree had borne the brunt of the damage, its branches snapped like spindly arms, hanging limp and broken, pale patches mottled its trunk where the storm had scraped the bark clean away.

All day, I thought about the mānuka tree and what it had endured, how it had stood up to the storm like a proud and weary sentry and against the dimming light, the lengthening shadows, I caught the sinking sun throwing the last of its fiery glow onto the raw, pale patches where the mānuka had been stripped, the tree, suddenly aflame, as though lit from within. I found myself touched by this moment of unexpected beauty. I thought, how strange it was for a living thing to be battered and broken, to remain quietly resolute. And aren't we all like that? Damaged and battle scarred, yet somehow luminous, the way the world can sometimes tilt our way for one miraculous moment and render our wounds into light.

Parallel Worlds

I believe in parallel worlds because you and I exist in every one of my stories, anywhere love blooms between two people, across space and time.

There is only me, and there is only you.

Concessions

With the passing of time, you find yourself in places you swore you'd never be. You make concessions for your dreams. No longer reach for the unattainable. For so long, I was afraid of this twilight place, afraid of my world contracting. But now I am here, I don't ever want to go back to how it was.

If I Were to Describe Love, It Would Be This

You watch me upload a video on Instagram, then delete it within the first few minutes. You tell me I have nothing to prove but I am already wracked with anxiety. I pore through my email, unsubscribe from mailing lists, check my spam folder in case there is something crucial I've missed. I add soap powder and toothpaste to my online shopping list. *Do you want anything?* I ask. You smile, *Only you.* I scrutinize my shopping cart, agonizing over what to remove, what to keep, adding and subtracting from my self-worth. And that night, as I lay awake, my brain chewing itself raw, full of worry, I woke you up and you, without a word, sat up and turned on the light, let me talk for as long as I had to.

The Soul of a Poet

Anyone can write a scene that stirs the imagination. A hand placed here, an elbow there, an open window and curtain billowing, a silhouette against a sunset wall—but it takes the soul of a poet to infuse these vignettes with feeling.

Absolution

True love does not absolve you, the way we were led to believe. Instead, it shines a light in every corner of your darkest self, all the troubled reflections of your psyche, broken things you never got around to fixing. It shakes out all your ghosts, asks you to confront the deepest parts of yourself. True love is a karmic force that will give and take in accordance with the universal ledger. At its core true love is Judgment, our highest calling. The sum of our deeds—both good and evil—will determine the breadth and time of this love.

Relationship

A healthy relationship is democratic. When you build a life with someone, you should have equal say in that life. You should be able to speak your mind freely, pursue a passion or career of your choosing. Have access to your own money. Be allowed to see your family and friends, without asking for permission. Being in a healthy relationship is about autonomy. Anything outside of this is unacceptable. Because domestic abuse takes on many forms, and not all of them are violent. But it doesn't mean they aren't harmful. If you sense something isn't right, then trust that instinct.

How Long

How long will you stay? he asks.
She answers, *For as long as there is poetry here.*

Paperweight

A verse on a gilded page, heavy as a heart. An old friend comes to the phone. I ask, *draw us a card.* I plead, *anything but the lovers—how can we ever be more if the romance refuses to die?* If I'm never allowed to fall out of your good graces, if I never get to see you one post-apocalyptic morning with smoke in your eyes, between the deluge of the day to day. Just a year ago, I was walking on your rooftop, howling at your window, beating down your door. You said, *stop trying to align the stars and wait—just wait for them to fall.*

First published in Invisible Strings: 113 Poets Respond to the Songs of Taylor Swift, *2024.*

The Bitter End

The act of reading a book will fall between two categories; one where the world around you melts into the words before you, until those words become indistinguishable from reality. When reading feels as natural as breathing. And then there are books you must grit your teeth to get through, where every line feels tedious, but you have resolved yourself to see it all the way to the bitter end. That's what we've become; another thing to get through.

My Ghosts

I hope to never lose the thing that keeps me centered, that balances me out. I know what it's like to spin out of control, to bang on the door of my past self, not being able to intervene. I know how it feels to be two wildly conflicting people inhabiting the same body. I envy those who are firmly anchored in themselves, who do not have this internal struggle. Those who are never haunted by the ghosts of their other selves.

So Close

Ask me where I was at the start of December, if I was anywhere near the dream you spun for me like cotton candy. It doesn't seem to matter to you, does it, that we were getting somewhere. I think I drove us straight into the wilderness that night we wound up lost but you wanted to keep driving. You said, *let's stay here until morning*. But I was afraid I'd never find my way back. And so, the sun never rose for us again, but for me, it will never stop setting. I kept you away from me, as far away as I could and still, you were so close.

On Read

There is a new message from him. If she leaves it unread, she could make time stand still. If she leaves it unread, she won't ever have to wonder if there will be another.

But she reads it anyway. She reads it and she waits.

And she waits and she waits.

Creativity and Passion

Creativity compels you. Passion drives you. The combination of these two things will make you unstoppable.

The Other Woman

I felt you pulling away, felt us growing apart, thought you were getting tired of my easy laughter, our idling conversations. The slow but steady withdrawal of your warmth and affection shook the foundation of all my dreams to the core. In my peripheral, I caught the shadow of another and found the courage to ask you if there was someone else. That was when I learned the devastating truth, that the whole time I was the other woman.

Shapes

We name things according to the shapes they inhabit. Starfruit, bellflowers, and candy hearts. And my love—a flimsy, moving thing, stretches around you, pulls you in like a lasso. It is only in the meeting of your heart that I have come to know the shape of my own.

Fool's Gold

You grew impatient
when the gods withheld.
Looked for alliances elsewhere.

You chose your deities
over the divine
and these imposters
showered you
with fool's gold.

Still Here

As a writer, you are judged, not by what you have written but what others write about you. But I am proud that I didn't give in to those critical voices. I'm proud that I never put my name to anything that wasn't mine. I am proud that despite what others callously took from me, I am still here.

Measure

The measure of a man is not in how he loves you but how he lets you go.

From a Place

Have you ever considered the possibility that the person you love the most in this world was the one tasked with writing your story? That your life was constructed from this love that has been with you from the onset and will remain with you throughout. That your story was written from a place of wanting everything for you.

Order

I was born into chaos, carried across a tide that threatened to turn at any moment. I have lived my whole life trying to establish order. Alphabetizing my books. Compartmentalizing my lovers. Putting pictures into boxes, shutting away parts of myself into drawers. Cataloging synchronicities. Creating schedules and spreadsheets, an endless list of longings I could never hope to check off. But all this pales in comparison to the discipline of writing. The act of organizing my thoughts. What makes better sense of disorder than that?

Crux

There is a wish for which I am waiting. So, I write poetry in my dreams. My life is a sentence I keep deconstructing. Yet, I still don't know how to name you. I think you are chaos, a whisper into the void. I think you are entropy—the world falling into ruin. I think you are the inevitable, the relentless forward motion of time. I think you are love, I think you are light, I think you are the crux of everything.

Well of Words

You must never compromise your sense of self for someone else's version of you. Do not put your own desires before what you know is right. You are the measure of your worth. When others take from you, let them. For their well of words has already run dry, while yours never will.

This Place of Refuge

Our love remains on neutral ground. Battles must be fought elsewhere.

Here we commune and muse about our other selves, the ugliness of our egos, words spoken in anger—we only know we don't mean them once they are said. We relinquish our greatest fears, acknowledge our wrongs, make apologies for the countless ways we have hurt each other; the foundations we have laid to ruin.

We dress each other's wounds, replenish our provisions. Go back to the battlefield with the knowledge we will always have this place of refuge in which we can return.

The Happiest

Maybe there is no other story beyond what is unfolding for you now. Maybe this moment isn't the present, but a place you have come back to, for it was here where you were the happiest.

When You Were Here

I found a postcard dated before I met you, a Ferris wheel set against a seascape and someone wishing me there. A relic from a time when I hadn't met you. I don't think of it so much these days. For such a long time, I was trying to process you, the way our dreams process our waking world. But all that's left are remnants of my despair, going through my days, patching together the semblance of a life. The physicality of your absence, always at my center, the gravity that tethers me to you. Maybe you loved me, however briefly. Maybe I'm not remembering things correctly—the distortion of memory and time like a word spoken underwater. How can a memory feel more real to me than the moment I lived it? How can your absence be more present, than when you were here?

Days Like This

Today, I asked a dozen questions, and everyone said *yes*. On the road, every traffic light said *go*, as though the universe had commanded it. I found myself in sync, reset to a cosmic timer. I moved through the world, with a lightness in my step. And everything was easy. I thought, *why can't every day be like this?* But the days of backlogs, dead ends, and stagnation are what make days like this so sweet.

If I Were to Leave

I think if I were to leave, I would be sad for a long time but eventually, I'd be happier than I am now.

Almost November

It is almost November, and I have been trying to reach you—if only you can hold on for a while longer. When I get there, everything will return to how it was. You can go back to carving out that dream with all the love and attention it deserves. Until then, know you haven't gone beyond the pale; I know how to keep you safe. Remember, curses can delay, but they cannot withhold. I draw hearts around your name, and everything is light. I walk without running, but I'm still making ground.

Acknowledgments

With all my heart, I want to thank my longtime editor and friend Patty Rice, with whom I've had the joy of creating thirteen books since 2013. Your wisdom, care, and unwavering belief in my work have been a blessing from the beginning. I will miss you dearly.

To Melissa, my new editor—thank you for embracing this book with warmth and insight. I am so grateful for your guidance as we begin this new journey together.

To my agent, Alec, my steadfast champion—thank you for always believing in my voice and helping to bring these words into the world.

To Kirsty, whose leadership and support have meant so much—thank you for everything you do behind the scenes, along with Kathy and the rest of the team at Andrews McMeel.

Thank you to Diane for your beautiful design work.

To Habin, who once saved Whiskey's life—your care and dedication mean more than words can express.

To Michael, thank you for your support, encouragement, and all the quiet ways you keep me going.

And finally, to my readers to whom I owe everything. I can never thank you enough.

Index